Inner Thoughts

Jody Peters

Presentation by *BookLeaf Publishing*

Web: www.bookleafpub.com

E-mail: info@bookleafpub.com

ISBN: 978-93-95755-18-4

First edition 2022

*This book is dedicated to my mom - Janice
(Wright) Unrau. Even though we did not get
along most of our lives, you showed me how to
be honest, if only with myself.*

About a Boy

Once upon a time
Not so long ago,
There was this boy

I didn't know him
I didn't like him
He threw mud at me, but
He paid attention to me

That's all I wanted
Attention

A trip to the beach
Or a simple conversation
Whatever it may be
He gave it to me

It wasn't right
It never will be
It happened
I realized what I'd done

With attention my only goal
I wasn't going anywhere
I'd been warned before

She said he was a jerk

I believed her

A week in time
I didn't want to come
I sat at home wondering
Just wondering

Will I be able to handle it?
The mud, the "abuse"
Should I even bother going?
HE is going to be there

THE WEEK:
A week of marshmallows and mud
Slip'n'slides and water fights
Something changed, but what?

All of a sudden there we were
You and me
Me and you
I don't understand it

I hated you
I honestly really hated you
But then I found I liked you
Why? I don't get it

I said it wouldn't work
I was scared
I didn't want to like you

You know my heart
It's been smashed so bad
Sometimes I wonder why it's still there

Then I remember God
He fixed it last time
I don't want to give it away again
Yet, somehow, I manage to

You never asked for it
In fact, you were quite polite
I gave it willingly
Please take care of it
It's more fragile than it looks

You are the sunshine on cloudy days
The one that makes the clouds go away
You make me feel on top of the world
When I feel at the bottom

You make me feel beautiful
Even if you're the only one that sees it.

Thank you for showing me
Life is what you make it

And not to let life make me
I love you

The First Time

Just a couple of teenagers
We just wanted to have some fun
We never thought we'd go that far
We'd only just begun

The first time it was scary
Scarier than I'd thought
The consequences could've been bad
Nothing that I'd want

It scared me half to death to think
Of what we'd done that night
And though we maybe wanted it
We knew it wasn't right

I told my mom and friend held dear
And got much-needed relief
You told your friends and cousin
And they told you to leave

We both had warnings from my sister
Whom I love so dear
Yet nonetheless, it happened twice
But this time with less fear

A bridge was crossed the first time through
"Again," we said, "no more"
But here there was another bridge
We crossed it like before

You said the first you could escape
The second becomes a rut
I believe you now and yet somehow
I still feel like a slut

I tell my mom most everything
But these she'll never know
For "if," she said, "it happens again
The boy will have to go"

I gave you something I can't take back
You did the very same
The choice was very mutual
I will not lay a blame

The bridge we crossed the other night
Makes everything seem new
What was, is no longer
It's been tried through and through

The reason I said yes last time
Is really rather easy
I was scared of what you'd think of me
It kind of made me queasy

My biggest fear in all my years
Has been a fear of man
You love me now, but if I say no
Will you love me then?

This is the question for which an answer
Is quite necessary
For if it's "no" the road ahead
Looks deep, dark, and scary

Memories of Love

Read through some old poems today
Found some which brightened the day
Found one especially true
Because it talked about you

It talked of memories I'll never forget
It talked of things I'll never regret
Places, people, things to do
Especially, it talked about you

I know poetry is not my best line
But it expresses thoughts from this heart of mine
My main thought (deeply heartfelt too);
I love you, Hun, I love you

Friends

Some are quiet
Some are obnoxious
Some are lazy
Some are industrious
But all are friends!

Some are boisterous
Some are relaxed
Some are supportive
Some drag others down
But all are friends!

Some are good listeners
Some are good talkers
Some are advisors
Some are excusers
But all are friends!

Each has different talents
Each has different abilities
Each has some sort of problem
Each has a group to help them
Because all are friends!

Cherish friends now

Soon paths will part
Build each other up
Don't tear anyone apart

Friends are precious
Friends are few
Learn to love them
But most of all
Be true

Friends as Family

I try to help you lovingly
You help me with great care
I feel like you're my family
We love going everywhere

"Family, they're not!" they say
But how do they really know?
My friends are here everyday
To show me where to go

If I ever lost you somehow
I'm not sure what I'd do
But I won't worry about that now
I'll just thank the Lord for you!

Thoughts

My thoughts are in such disarray
I need some time to think and pray
I feel like I am such a clown
Never knowing up from down

I'm grieving and happy in the same breath
Oh, what on earth will come up next?
My anger gets the better of me
When stupid things do I see

Am I a good wife or a good mother?
Am I a good daughter to my father?
What about teacher? Mentor? Friend?
I think my confidence needs a mend

At Jesus' feet, I leave my thoughts
So by Satan, I won't be caught
Now I must pray and ask for guidance
In Jesus alone, I find my confidence

Identity Crisis

Dark and dim
Far away, thin
Someone else has taken me
To where I must not go

Can it be?
Why?
Who am I?
Questions scorch my brain

Will I ever return from that place
So far away, so out of reach?
Will I see reality?
Stop living this dream
Complacency running through me
Like a waterfall

I'm not here
But then who am I?
Where did I go?
When come I back?

If you see me, I'm no different
You can't tell
I'm missing my life

But if you saw
My brain
My thoughts
My feelings
You'd understand

I'm not the same as I was
I want to feel something.
Pain, disgust, regret,
Anything

Is that how I changed?
Needing to feel something
But Love not found

I know the right answers
At least I thought I did
Now, the wrong is right, but still
The pain won't come

How far will it go?
What mental torture must I endure?
What temptations?
What consequences?

When will I realize
I could lose it all
And that which is

Shouldn't be

I am not myself
Reading, distracted
Love, pain,
guilt, shame
Loss is not what I want

When will it end?
Will I lose him first?

I can feel God changing me
Bringing me back
Slowly
God? How long?

Do I want to change?
Deep down, yes
On the surface, no

Tears shed
Relationships lost?
Damaged anyways
Love? Unattainable.

Slowly, I feel disgust
Slowly, I feel pain
Slowly, I feel guilt
Slowly, I feel...

Loss

Have I lost my chance?
Is there forgiveness for this?
What can I do now?
Where do I go?

Forward.

Free

17

Have you ever had a captive feeling in your
brain?
You want to be yourself but you're afraid?
I believe that we all go through this at least once
Maybe we can try and push our fear aside

I wanna be free
I wanna let myself go
Let the world know
Who I am
I wanna be free

Your parents tell you to be yourself
But is that what they really want?
I think that they want us to be ourselves
With their own mind

I wanna be free
I wanna let myself go
Let the world know
Who I am
I wanna be free

If people knew just who I was deep down inside

I would be way less afraid and maybe I wouldn't
hide...

I wanna be free
I wanna let myself go
Let the world know
Who I am
I wanna be free

Maybe... just maybe
There is a way around it
God can... yes God can
Help us through the riot

I can be free!
I can let myself go
Let the world know
Who I am
I can be free!

Through the Clouds

She was sitting with her friends
And then it didn't feel right
She was so confused
She couldn't concentrate that night

She had just made some new friends
But she got a little scared
She didn't get too close
In case nobody cared

She couldn't see through the clouds
There was something in her way
All that she ever needed
She thought You had turned away

It wasn't the first time
Suicide was on her mind
Deep down inside she knew
There was another way through

She couldn't see through the clouds
There was something in her way
All that she ever needed
She thought You had turned away

Then she got to thinking
Maybe You were still there
Her confidence need not be taken
Because You are everywhere

She couldn't see through the clouds
There'd been something in her way
All that she'd ever needed
She knows that You're here to stay

Change

Change is eternal
How else do we grow?
We cannot fathom
What we do not know

The universe creator
God up above
Holds the whole world
Secure in His love

He's not affected
By any surprise
for He has created
Every sunrise

Though change is eternal
My hope rests in this;
God knows what He's doing
because He was, will be, and is.

Awkwardness

Why do we skip through the awkward?
It just sits there, left alone
No one willing to acknowledge it

When you are prayed for
Act like this
Why?

We don't talk about that subject
Why not?

Muscle through
Act the part
Hope they don't see through you
Why?

Home

This is not my home
I wanna go where I belong
To the place I call my own
To be accepted and Loved

Lord, you know
I want to be with you for all my days
Eternally praise you
But this is not my home

Being here on earth
I've learned a lot
About love and faith and trust
And who You are

When I close my eyes I dream
Of how it's meant to be
All of Heaven is smiling

It's when I wake up that I know
The world has go to change somehow
And it won't do it alone

I pick up my cross
Thank my Lord for what He did

I move on out in His accord
To set the world free

I couldn't do it without Him.
I know. I've tried.
But I can do anything
When He is on my side

I try to imagine what Jesus will say
When I enter Heaven's gates
Will he say "well done, my daughter"
Or just a simple "thank-you"?

I hear the angels say
Welcome here
This is your home
You were dead but now you're alive
This is where you belong

We were watching you
Guarding you
Thanking Him each day
And although we missed you then
You're here now
And you're here to stay

And I sing
This is my home
This is where I belong

I could only sense it then
But now I know
This is home

You Are Here

Dear Lord, I missed you
I'm sorry for running away
Please come and take me
Lead me in Your way

Dear Lord, I need you
I need you every day
I've tried life without you
There is no other way

I cannot understand
I will never comprehend
Why you love
Why you care

You are the only one
Who knows my heart
Inside and out

You are the only one
I can run to
In the dark

You are amazing
You never fail me
No matter where I am
Lord, You are here

Here I Am

Here I am
Standing here alone again
Here I am
Waiting to see the Son again

It's been so long
So hard
It's wearing me down
I need to see
To know that I am Yours

I cry out to you
Once again
You are my rock
When I'm standing in the sand

You lift me up
When I need the strength to fly
I am yours

Here I am
Standing here in your presence
Here I am
With the Son of man

God, You are my life
I surrender everything
Have my heart
Take it all and show me Your power

I am Yours

Gone too Soon

You took him away
Left the family astray
Why did You do it?
God, what is Your plan?

Where are you going with this?
Leaving us in distress
It's too much to comprehend
We do not understand

How could this by Your plan?
We really don't understand
Can You give us a sign
To know that You still care

Somewhere, somehow we know that
You have a plan for us
Whatever it is Lord
We will submit in love, but

He'll never see his kids through high school
He'll never walk them down the aisle
He'll never see his kids grow up
To be who You want them to be

His kids have lost a father
His wife has lost a best friend
His parents lost a son
Lord, why put them through all this?

Identity in Christ

When will they see You?
How will they know?
Who will go teach them
If we do not go?

Cultures are shifting
This land's not the same
Your love for your people
Will always remain

We're YOUR sons and daughters
Your vessels, Your kids
Yet we're out here living
Like this is all there is

Take us and shape us
To who You want us to be
Train us to live
Like children of the King

If we are not different
From everyone else
We may as well be
A trinket on a shelf

This world is fleeting
Our time here is short
We need to know
We need Your support

When we know we are Yours
Our thinking will change
Our actions will follow
Our lives rearrange

Without You this life
Does not have a point
We need You, please teach us
You don't disappoint

Send us, we're willing
We will not say no
Show us and teach us
Where we ought to go

We are Your children
Your family at best
Until we realize this
We will not be at rest

You are our Father
Holy and good
This is a trait
That MUST be understood

Music

Universal
Pleasant
Awe-inspiring

Difficult
Easier than poetry - for me

Music changes people
Shifts atmospheres
Calms nerves
Unites

Without music
Where would we be?
Who would we be?
Who would I be?

Happy Place

Sun
Water
Rocks

The air wisping threw the nearby trees
Colours more vibrant than life
Peace more tangible than sand
God more real than grass

This. This is my happy place

Seasons

SPRING
New life
New promise
Potential at its greatest

I bring the end of hibernation
Neighbours finally see each other

I'm the butterfly breaking out of the cocoon
I bring families together to celebrate the love of
Jesus

I'm the best.
I am Spring.

SUMMER
I seem to be everyone's favourite
My days are long
My nights are short

I'm the extra-short, extra-fun person you want at
a party
I bring families together to relax and celebrate
their nation
I'm the best.

I am Summer.

FALL
Harvest
New beginnings
New chapters
School begins and routines resume

I'm the one who keeps everyone organized
I bring families together to celebrate the
abundance of God's provision

I'm the best.
I am Fall.

WINTER
Sneak attack
Storms
Snow
Resolutions and goals
Valentines

I'm the unpredictable friend that provides stark
change for good measure
I bring people together to celebrate the birth of
our Lord and Saviour, Jesus Christ.

I'm the best.
I am Winter.

God in Nature

In the quiet of the morning
As I look around the place
I can see Your glory
In many a wonderous space

The snow is a reflection of your brilliance
The trees are a show of your strength and power
The evergreen speaks of constancy
As does the blooming of each flower

People are a mirror of intelligence
Although a cloudy image they are
Each aspect of the creation
Gives a clue about the Creator's power

The thunder and lightning
Are mirrors of power
The rain is a picture of cleansing
Like stepping right out of the shower

You are truly awesome, God
Your creation clearly declares it
And as your daughter, Lord
I want to be fully aware of it